What is a king?
What should he do?
Is a ruler what you
want to be?

Let me compare two
kings for you,
And you decide
which is royalty.

One king is born in a castle tall,
With servants and handmaids to claim.

The other is born in a stable small,
With nothing to ever bring Him
fame.

The first king is taught by scholars wise,
All the laws and edicts ever made.

The other,
taught by his father, tries
To learn an honest carpenter's
trade.

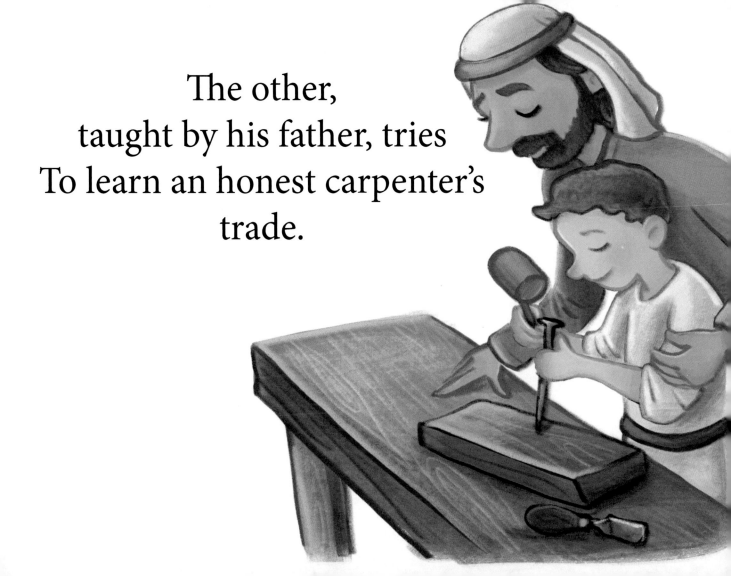

One has riches
and fancy clothes,
To impress with his
finest array.

One wears homespun
and kindly shows,
The downtrodden
people to pray.

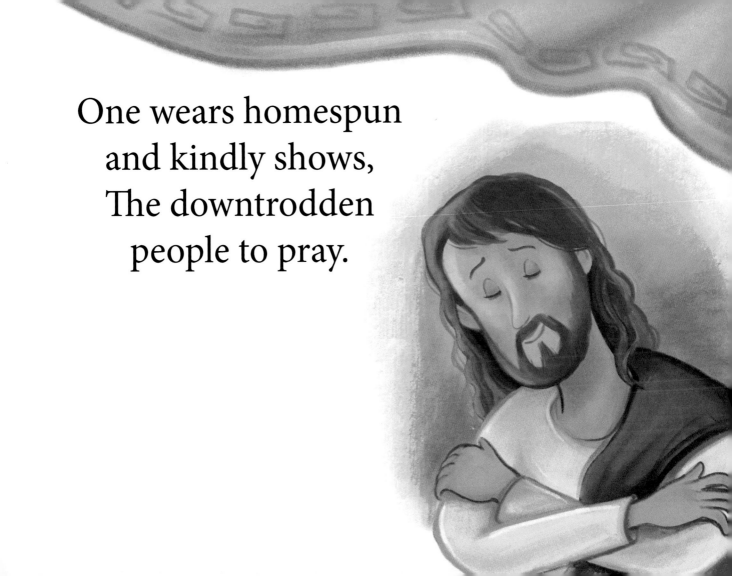

King one wears a crown of gold on his head;
His subjects bow down at his sight.

King two wore a crown fo thorns instead,
Was mocked, spat on, treated with spite.

One king tells everyone
what to do,
Giving no chance to deviate.

The other by His example true
Taught each could choose his
own fate.

One king has
gold and can pay
any price,
But to others he
does not give.

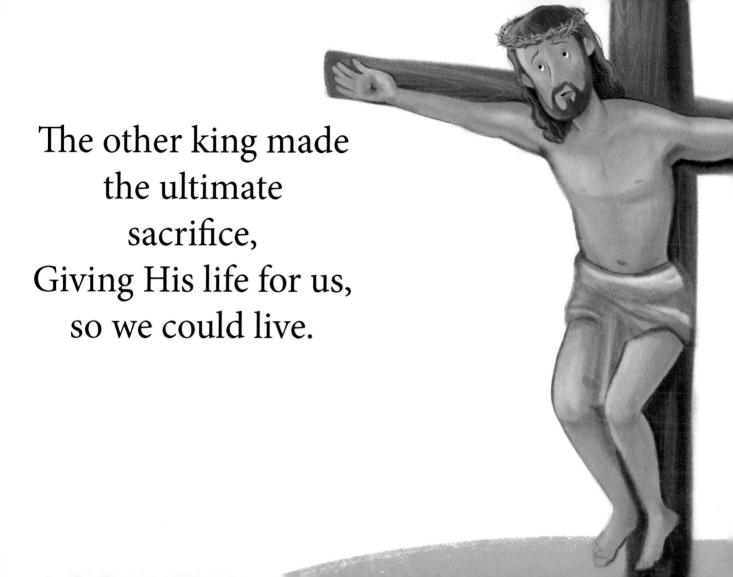

The other king made
the ultimate
sacrifice,
Giving His life for us,
so we could live.

Which of these two kings
is the one
You would consider of royal
birth?

The one who rules his current kingdom?
Or the one who will rule the whole Earth?

Wealth and power does not make kings,
Being ruled does not bring us love.

But being taught the sacred things,
We'll return to our Father above.

The second king is God's own Son,
Sent to teach the gospel way.

He taught us that
everyone
Can live with Him
one day.

The End!

Made in the USA
Middletown, DE
25 October 2021